LIVING THINGS

FOOD CHAINS AND WEBS

Anita Ganeri

Heinemann
LIBRARY

www.heinemann.co.uk
Visit our website to find out more information about Heinemann Library books.

To order:

 Phone 44 (0) 1865 888066

 Send a fax to 44 (0) 1865 314091

 Visit the Heinemann Bookshop at www.heinemann.co.uk to browse our catalogue and order online.

First published in Great Britain by Heinemann Library, Halley Court, Jordan Hill, Oxford OX2 8EJ a division of Reed Educational and Professional Publishing Ltd. Heinemann is a registered trademark of Reed Educational & Professional Publishing Ltd.

OXFORD MELBOURNE AUCKLAND
JOHANNESBURG BLANTYRE GABORONE
IBADAN PORTSMOUTH (NH) USA CHICAGO

Designed by Celia Floyd
Illustrations by Alan Fraser
Originated by Dot Gradations
Printed in Hong Kong/China

ISBN 0 431 10925 7 (hardback)
06 05 04 03 02 01
10 9 8 7 6 5 4 3 2

ISBN 0 431 10932 X (paperback)
06 05 04 03 02 01
10 9 8 7 6 5 4 3 2 1

British Library Cataloguing in Publication Data

Ganeri, Anita
   Food chains and webs. – (Living things)
   1. Food chains (Ecology) – Juvenile literature
   I. Title
   577.1′6

Acknowledgements

The Publishers would like to thank the following for permission to reproduce photographs:

Bruce Coleman Collection: Jeff Foott pg.10, Andrew Purcell pg.19, Sir Jeremy Grayson pg.26; *FLPA*: E & D Hosking; *NHPA*: Ralph & Daphne Keller pg.4, Rod Planck pg.5, Nigel J Dennis pg.8, Michael Leach pg.9, Jany Sauvanet pg.11, Kevin Schafer pg.12, T Kitchin & V Hurst pg.13, Martin Harvey pg.13, Mark Bowler pg.17, Bill Wood pg.21, Laurie Campbell pg.22, B Jones & M Shimlock pg.23, B & C Alexander pg.24, Hellio & Van Ingen pg.28, R Sorensen & J Olsen pg.29; *Oxford Scientific Films*: Daniel J Cox pg.15, Michael Fogden pg.16.

Cover photograph reproduced with permission of Oxford Scientific Films.

Every effort has been made to contact copyright holders of any material reproduced in this book. Any omissions will be rectified in subsequent printings if notice is given to the Publisher.

Any words appearing in the text in bold, **like this**, are explained in the glossary.

Contents

Introduction

The six books in this series explore the world of living things. *Food Chains and Webs* looks at how plants and animals are linked together by what they eat. It shows how nearly all food chains start with green plants because green plants can make their own food.

Food and feeding

All living things need food to stay alive. Food gives them **energy** to make new **cells**, grow and stay healthy. Green plants make their own food by **photosynthesis** (see page 5). Animals cannot make their own food. They have to hunt for food to eat. Some animals eat plants. Some animals eat other animals.

Sheep grazing on grass.

Plants and animals

A **habitat** is a place where plants and animals live. All the plants and animals in a habitat are linked by what they eat. The links join up to make a food chain. Each link in the chain is food for the next in line. Some food chains are quite simple. In the Arctic, fish eat sea plants. Then seals eat the fish. Then polar bears eat the seals. Different food chains join together to make a food web.

Plant food

Green plants start off nearly every food chain. This is because they can make their own food. Animals then eat the plants. Plants are called **producers** because they make, or produce, food. Animals that eat plants are called **primary consumers**. Animals that eat plant-eating animals are called **secondary consumers**.

Making food

Green plants make food in their leaves. This is called photosynthesis. The leaves contain a green **chemical** called **chlorophyll**. It soaks up sunlight and uses it to turn **carbon dioxide** gas from the air and water from the ground into food. **Oxygen** gas is given off as waste.

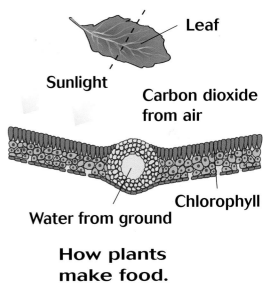

Leaf

Sunlight

Carbon dioxide from air

Chlorophyll

Water from ground

How plants make food.

Did you know?
Many plants have special features to stop them being eaten. Cacti grow in the desert. They have prickly spines instead of leaves. The prickles help keep hungry animals away.

A saguaro cactus.

How food chains work

Living things are linked by what they eat. For example, snails eat plants. Then birds eat the snails. Next a fox might eat a bird. In this way, the **energy** made by green plants when they make their own food is passed along the food chain. Nearly all food chains start with a plant and end with an animal. Animals that eat other animals are called **predators**. The animals they eat are called **prey**.

Food webs

Animals often eat a mixture of foods. So an animal can appear in many different food chains. When several food chains join up together, they form a food web. Our example food chain (plant - snail - bird - fox) is part of a big woodland food web like the one below. How many food chains can you find? Which animals are predators and which are prey?

A woodland food web.

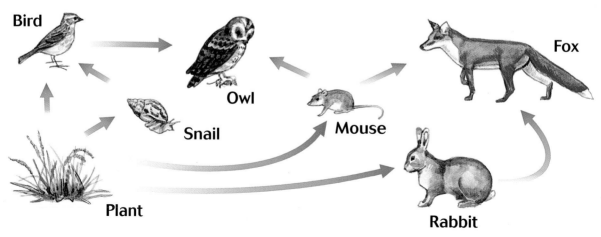

Pyramid of numbers

You can use a diagram called a pyramid to show the number of living things in a food chain. Usually there are more plants than prey, and more prey than predators. For example, in the pyramid below, there are more plants than snails (prey), and more snails than birds (predators). Otherwise the snails and birds would go hungry.

A pyramid of numbers.

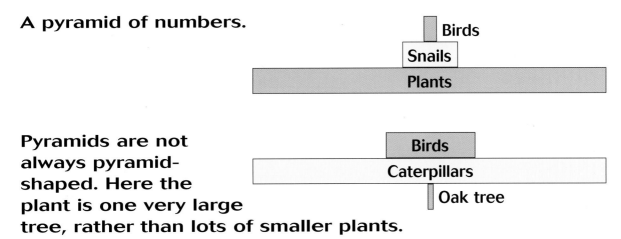

Pyramids are not always pyramid-shaped. Here the plant is one very large tree, rather than lots of smaller plants.

Pyramid of biomass

You can use another pyramid to show the amount of living things in a food chain. This is called a **pyramid of biomass**. The pyramid below shows how big and heavy the oak tree is. This is called its biomass. The biomass of the oak tree is much bigger than the caterpillars that feed on it.
The biomass of the caterpillars is much bigger than that of the birds.

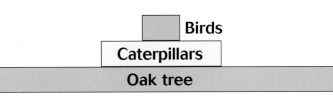

A pyramid of biomass.

Herbivores

Herbivores are animals that only eat plants. Some herbivores are tiny, such as insects that feed on plant juices. Others are huge, such as elephants that can uproot whole trees. The plants they eat are not very nourishing. So herbivores need to spend a lot of their lives eating to get enough **energy** to stay alive. They often have to compete with other herbivores for food.

Giraffes eating leaves.

Grassland plant-eaters

Many different herbivores live in **grasslands**. They can live together because each animal eats different plants. In Africa, giraffes and elephants mainly eat the leaves from trees and bushes. Zebras and antelopes mainly eat grass.

Did you know?

African elephants are herbivores. They spend eighteen hours a day eating. They have enormous appetites. In one day, an adult elephant may eat more than 225 kilograms of leaves, bark and flowers. Some elephants eat twice that much.

Eating seeds

Many birds are herbivores. They eat fruit, nuts and seeds. The size and shape of their beaks help them to reach their food. Some birds have short, sharp beaks for opening seeds. Parrots have very strong beaks for cracking nuts. They use the hooked end for scooping the soft insides out of fruit. Crossbills have crossed-over beaks for pulling seeds out of pine cones.

A crossbill.

Nectar drinkers

Insects feed on every part of a plant – the roots, stem, leaves and flowers. Caterpillars eat plant leaves. They can easily strip a plant bare. Butterflies eat a sweet liquid called nectar from inside flowers. They use a long, hollow tube to suck up the nectar.

Not being eaten

Many herbivores are eaten by other animals. To avoid being eaten, some herbivores simply run or fly away. Others have special features to protect them. Some have special patterns or markings to hide them from enemies. Others have poisonous skin or stings.

9

Carnivores

Carnivores are animals that only eat meat. They are the **predators** in a food chain. Carnivores have sharp, pointed teeth and claws for killing and tearing their **prey**. Shrews are small carnivores. They use up **energy** very quickly. They have to eat their own weight in food each day to get enough energy. Big carnivores, like lions, use energy more slowly. They need to eat much less for their size.

Hunting in packs

Wolves mostly feed on large **mammals** such as deer and moose. They have large dagger-like front teeth for gripping their prey. They hunt their prey in groups called packs. The pack is very well organized. It has a plan of attack to follow when it is hunting.

Grey wolves eating a deer.

Anteaters

The giant anteater has a long, pointed snout and a long, sticky tongue for catching ants and **termites**. The anteater tears open an ants' nest with its sharp claws. Then it flicks its tongue in and out to lap up the ants. The anteater eats about 30,000 ants a day.

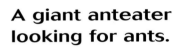

A giant anteater looking for ants.

Insect carnivores

Many insects are meat-eaters too. Robber flies perch on twigs, then pounce on other insects as they fly past. Robber flies have hairy faces. This stops their faces being stung by their prey.

Eating scraps

Some carnivores eat dead animals. Vultures in Africa eat animals killed by lions or cheetahs. The vultures fly overhead until the lions have eaten their fill. Then they pick at the scraps.

Did you know?

Some plants are carnivores. The Venus fly-trap makes its own food but it also eats meat. The fly-trap has leaves that are hinged together. They lie open, waiting for an insect to land. Then they snap shut.

Omnivores

Omnivores are animals that eat plants and other animals. They include bears, rats, pigs, chimpanzees and human beings. Omnivores eat many different types of food. This means that they can usually find plenty to eat. If they cannot find one type of food, they simply eat something else.

A mixed diet

Bears eat a very mixed diet. They eat fruit, leaves, nuts, honey, small **mammals** and fish. Spectacled bears from South America eat more than 80 different types of food. For example, they eat deer, birds, rabbits, fruit, flowers, cacti and moss.

A spectacled bear feeding on leaves.

Did you know?
Cockroaches usually eat dead or rotting plants. But in some places, cockroaches live in kitchens and eat scraps of food and household rubbish. Cockroaches can easily spread diseases.

Chimpanzee hunters

Chimpanzees eat leaves, buds, seeds, eggs and **termites**. They are also fierce hunters. They hunt in groups for monkeys and wild pigs in the forest. The meat is shared out among the whole group.

A chimpanzee digging for ants.

City living

Some omnivores have to change what they eat. Red foxes now live in many towns and cities, as well as in the countryside. They make their dens in parks and gardens. They hunt rabbits, birds and small **rodents**. They also raid dustbins for people's leftovers.

Raccoons raid dustbins in North America.

Fussy eaters

The giant panda is a fussy eater. It mostly eats bamboo stems, branches and leaves. It has to spend up to fifteen hours a day feeding to get enough food to survive. This is because it can only **digest** a small part of all the bamboo it eats. Giant pandas also eat rats, fish and rodents.

13

Woodland food chains

Woods and forests grow all over the world. Many animals feed on the trees and plants that grow in them. Some woods contain mainly trees like pines and spruces. These are called **coniferous** trees. Other woods contain trees like oaks and sycamores. They are called **deciduous** trees. There are many woodland food chains.

Forest food web

The Eastern Mixed Forest is a huge woodland in the USA. It is a mixture of coniferous and deciduous trees. The trees include maples, beeches and pines. Many animals feed among the trees.

A mixed forest food web.

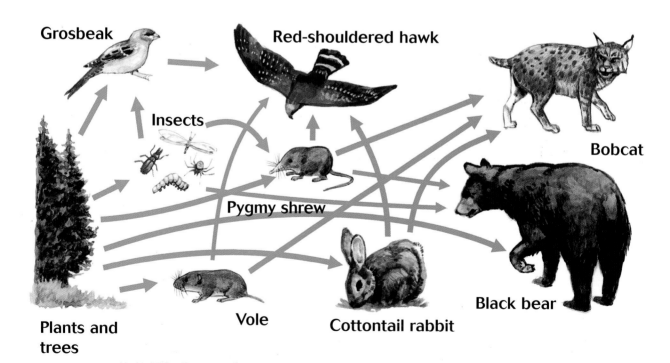

Grosbeak

Red-shouldered hawk

Insects

Bobcat

Pygmy shrew

Black bear

Plants and trees

Vole

Cottontail rabbit

Life in a oak tree

An oak tree provides food for thousands of woodland animals. Caterpillars and beetles eat oak leaves. Birds eat the caterpillars and beetles. Birds, voles and squirrels eat acorns. Even the dead leaves on the ground are food for woodlice, worms and small **mammals**. Owls live in the branches and hunt mice and voles.

Forests in winter

In autumn, the leaves of deciduous trees change colour to red, yellow and orange. Then the trees lose their leaves. This helps the trees to survive the winter when it is difficult to make food. But it means less food for woodland animals. Some animals **hibernate** until spring. Others live off stores of nuts.

Did you know?
Koalas live in Australia. They eat eucalytpus leaves. Koalas can eat more than 1 kilogram of leaves and bark in a day. They even smell of eucalyptus!

A koala eating eucalyptus leaves.

Rainforest food chains

Rainforests are home to at least half of all the types of plants and animals on Earth yet they only cover a small part of the land. Rainforests grow in layers, based on how tall the trees grow. The layers are the forest floor, the understorey, the canopy and the emergent layer. Each layer has its own plants and animals, and its own food chains. Many rainforest animals live in the canopy. It is like a thick green roof of leaves over the rainforest.

On the forest floor

The forest floor is dark and gloomy. It is covered in dead leaves. These rot away and their goodness soaks back into the soil. Many small creatures, such as insects and millipedes, eat the rotting leaves. Small **mammals** feed on the insects. In turn they are **prey** for larger animals, such as jaguars.

Did you know?
The rainforest flower on the right is really an insect. It is called a flower mantis. It looks just like a flower. Even its wings look like petals. This helps it to catch its prey, without being seen.

A flower mantis.

Beware – poison

The arrow-poison frog lives in the understorey and canopy. It mainly eats insects. But it also has enemies. To avoid being eaten by snakes and birds, the frog has deadly poisonous skin. The frog's bright colours warn its enemies that it is very nasty to eat.

Monkey-eating eagles

Monkey-eating eagles make their nests in the tallest trees. These trees grow in the emergent layer. The eagles are fierce hunters. They fly through the branches looking for monkeys to eat. Then the eagles take their prey back to their nest.

A monkey-eating eagle.

Rainforest plant-eaters

Many rainforest animals feed on the rainforest trees. An orang-utan mainly eats rainforest fruits such as figs, mangoes, lychees and durian fruit. The orang-utans can remember exactly where to find each particular type of tree in the forest.

An orang-utan.

Freshwater food chains

Only about three per cent of all the water on Earth is **fresh**. Fresh water is found in rivers, ponds, lakes and marshes. Each place has its own food chains and webs. A freshwater food chain starts with water plants. Tiny **invertebrates**, such as insects and snails, eat the plants. Fish and larger animals, such as birds, eat the invertebrates.

Pond plants

All freshwater animals rely on plants for their food. Some pond plants grow around the pond edges. Other plants grow on the surface of the water or underwater. Pond plants include huge waterlilies and tiny water weeds. They also give shelter to the animals in the pond.

A pond food chain.

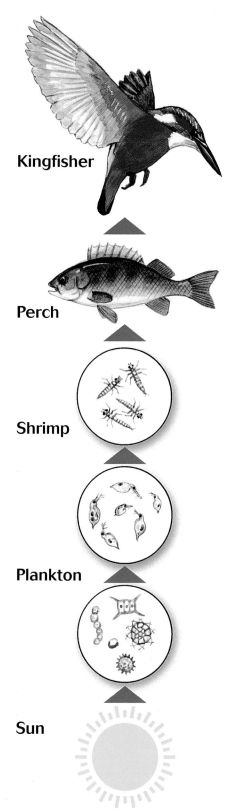

Kingfisher

Perch

Shrimp

Plankton

Sun

Going fishing

Many birds eat freshwater fish. Some birds have special feet and beaks to help them catch their food. Herons have long legs for wading into the water. They have long, pointed beaks for stabbing their **prey**.

Feeding underwater

The duck-billed platypus lives in rivers and streams in Australia. It dives underwater. Then it scoops up food from the river bed with its bill. The platypus eats insects, shellfish and worms. It stores the food in its cheeks until it comes to the surface and eats it.

A dragonfly larva eating a worm.

Dragonfly diet

Many different insects live near fresh water. Some insects are eaten by fish and birds. Other insects are fierce hunters. Dragonfly **larvae** live underwater. They hunt water fleas, worms, tadpoles and small fish.

Did you know?

Piranha fish live in the Amazon River. Many piranhas are fierce hunters with razor-sharp teeth. They usually eat dead or injured fish. But they can strip an animal as large as a cow to the bone in just a few minutes. Other piranhas eat fruit and leaves.

Ocean food chains

Salty water covers about two-thirds of the Earth. It lies in the oceans and seas. An enormous number of plants and animals live in the oceans. They are joined together in thousands of different food chains. These food chains make up one huge ocean food web.

Ocean plants

Every ocean food chain starts with tiny plants. The plants have only one **cell** in their bodies. They grow near the surface of the sea. Without these plants, nothing could live in the sea. Tiny sea animals graze on the plants. Larger animals eat the smaller ones.

An ocean food chain.

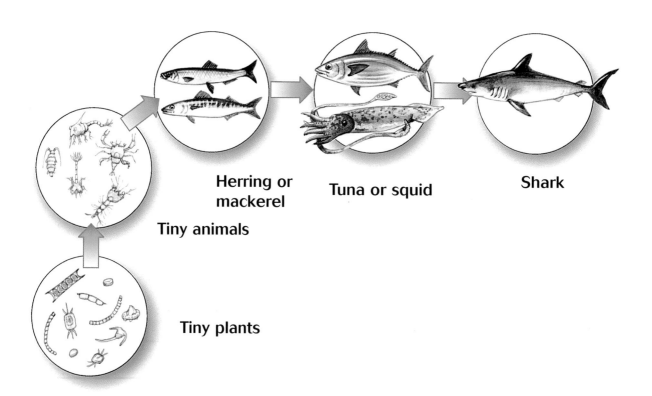

Herring or mackerel

Tuna or squid

Shark

Tiny animals

Tiny plants

Giant appetite

Some of the biggest animals in the sea eat some of the smallest ones. The blue whale is huge. But it eats tiny, shrimp-like animals called **krill**. A whale can eat up to 4 tonnes of krill a day. It uses its mouth like a sieve to catch the krill.

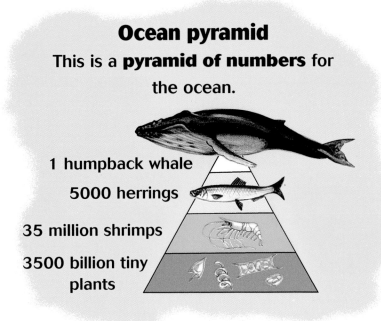

Ocean pyramid

This is a **pyramid of numbers** for the ocean.

1 humpback whale

5000 herrings

35 million shrimps

3500 billion tiny plants

Deep-sea features

It is dark and cold in the deep sea. No plants can grow there because there is no sunlight for making food. This means that there is very little food for other creatures. Many deep-sea animals have special features for catching as much food as possible. For example, gulper eels have huge mouths and stretchy stomachs for swallowing food.

Did you know?

Sea cucumbers live on the seabed and eat tiny scraps of food. To escape from enemies, sea cucumbers shoot out sticky guts. This tangles up their attacker.

A sea cucumber.

Seashores and reefs

Twice a day, the sea floods on to the shore. Then it flows out again. These changes in sea-level are called the tides. Most seashore animals look for food when the tide has gone out.

Seaweed

Seaweed clings to rocks along the shore. When the sea comes in, it floats on the surface. Then it can soak up sunlight for making food. Sea snails and other small creatures feed on the seaweed.

Shore birds

Shore birds feed on the shore when the tide is out. Some shore birds have short, strong beaks for opening up shells. Other shore birds have long, curved beaks for digging in the mud for worms and shellfish.

A shore bird looking for food.

Coral reefs

Thousands of creatures live on coral reefs. There are brightly coloured fish, octopuses and giant clams. Each creature has its own place on the reef. This is where it lives and feeds. Some animals eat the coral itself. Parrot fish scrape away at the coral with their beak-like mouths. Then they crunch the coral up.

A coral reef.

Coral builders

Coral reefs are built by tiny sea animals. They are related to jellyfish and sea anemones. They have stinging tentacles for catching their **prey**. They make stony cases around their soft bodies. When they die, the cases are left behind. Coral only grows in shallow water where there is plenty of Sun. This is because it grows together with sea plants which need the sunlight to make food.

Did you know?
Starfish are eating the Great Barrier Reef in Australia. A starfish grips a piece of coral. Then it pushes its stomach out of its body to cover the coral. It **digests** the coral and pulls its stomach back in.

Food chains and you

What have you eaten today? A pizza?
A sandwich? A cheese salad? A bowl of cereal?
Like all living things, you are part of lots of food
chains. Many
humans are
omnivores.
They eat both
plants and
animals. Some
people only eat
plants. They
are called
vegetarians.

Fishing
for food.

A balanced diet

You need to eat a mixture of food for **energy** and
goodness. This is called a balanced diet. The
different types of food you need are:
Carbohydrates – found in bread, rice and cereals.
Proteins – found in meat, fish, eggs and beans.
Fats – found in milk, cheese, butter and oils.
Vitamins – found in fruit, vegetables, fish
and milk.
Minerals – found in fish, vegetables, fruit and milk.
Fibre – found in fruit, vegetables, wholemeal
bread and bran.

Two food chains

If you eat a tuna fish sandwich, you become part of two food chains.

1 Sea plants – tiny sea animals – small fish - tuna fish – you

2 Wheat (the wheat is made into bread) – you

Vegetarians

Vegetarians are people that do not eat meat or fish. They think it is wrong to kill or harm animals. Vegetarians mainly eat vegetables, fruit, nuts, pulses such as lentils and beans, and grains such as wheat. Some eat eggs and dairy products because this does not mean killing animals. Here is what the food chains for a vegetarian cheese salad would look like:

1 Grass – cow (the cow's milk is made into vegetarian cheese) – you

2 Salad vegetables (plants) – you

Cycles in nature

Nothing is wasted in nature. Everything is used again and again. When living things die, their bodies rot away. The goodness from their bodies soaks into the soil. Plants use this goodness to grow. Animals eat the plants. When the plants and animals die, the whole cycle begins again.

Rich soils

Some living things feed on dead plants and animals. They are called **decomposers**. They are very important in food chains. They break down the bodies of dead plants and animals. Then the goodness from the dead bodies soaks into the ground. It makes the soil richer for more plants to grow.

Fungi on a tree trunk.

Feeding fungi

Fungi are not plants or animals. They belong to another group of living things. Fungi feed on dead material, such as dead leaves or rotting tree trunks. A fungus is made of tiny threads. The threads grow over the food. They **dissolve** the food, then they soak it up.

Carbon cycle

Carbon is found in all living things and is used again and again. This is called the carbon cycle.

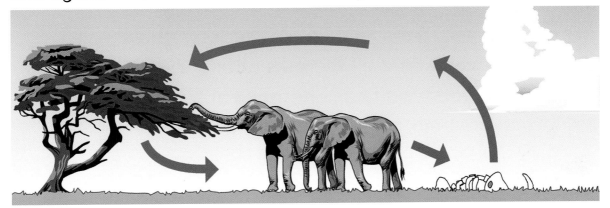

1 **Carbon dioxide** in the air.
2 Plants use carbon dioxide to make food.
3 Animals get carbon from the plants they eat.
4 Animals use carbon to grow and for **energy**.
5 Animals make waste and die.
6 Decomposers feed on the dead bodies. They also give off carbon dioxide in breathing.

Nitrogen cycle

Living things also need **nitrogen** to grow. This is what the nitrogen cycle looks like.

1 Plants take in **nitrates** from the soil.
2 Plants use nitrogen from the nitrates to grow.
3 Plants die and are broken down into **ammonium** compounds.
4 Animals also eat the plants.
5 Animal waste is broken down into ammonium compounds.
6 **Bacteria** in the soil turn the ammonium into nitrates.

27

Upsetting the balance

There is a good balance of plants and animals in a food chain. This means that there is enough for everyone to eat. But if one link in the food chain is broken, it can affect all the other living things. In a simple pond food chain, herons eat frogs that eat insects that eat plants. But if the insects died, the frogs would not have enough to eat. Then the herons could not eat the frogs.

When things go wrong

Poison can pass through a food chain. It gets stronger and stronger as it goes along. A **chemical** called **DDT** used to be sprayed on farmers' fields. It killed insects that ate the crops. But the rain washed the DDT into rivers and seas. It was taken up by tiny plants. Tiny animals ate the plants and fish ate the animals. Then birds of **prey**, like ospreys, ate the fish. Many ospreys died.

An osprey in its nest.

Poisoned shellfish

The metal mercury is deadly poisonous if it gets into a food chain. In 1952, a factory in Japan leaked mercury into the sea. It poisoned the shellfish. Many people ate the poisoned shellfish and died.

Competition for food

All animals need to eat to stay alive. But animals often have to **compete** for food. If there is lots of food in a place, more animals that live there will get enough to eat. But if lots of animals are competing for small amounts of food, some of the animals will starve.

Did you know?
Lemmings are **rodents** from Norway. They eat grass, moss and shrubs. Lemmings breed very quickly. This makes it difficult to get enough to eat. Sometimes the lemmings make a mad dash from home to look for food. Many die on the journey. This leaves the other lemmings with more to eat.

A lemming.

Conclusion

All living things need food to grow and keep their bodies healthy. Food passes from one living thing to another in a food chain. Each plant and animal is a vital link in the chain. You too are a link in many food chains. Just think what you have eaten today!

Glossary

ammonium   a chemical made from a mixture of nitrogen and other chemicals

bacteria   tiny living things that are found almost everywhere. They are decomposers.

carbon   a vitally important chemical substance found in the bodies of all living things

carbon dioxide   a gas found in the air. Plants and animals give off carbon dioxide when they breathe.

carnivore   an animal that only eats other animals

cell   a tiny building block that makes up the body of all living things

chemical   a substance found as a solid, liquid or gas

chlorophyll   green colouring found in plants. It helps the plants to make their own food.

compete   to struggle with something else

coniferous   trees like pine trees that produce cones

DDT   a poisonous chemical sprayed on farmers' crops to kill insect pests

deciduous   trees that regularly lose their leaves

decomposers   living things that break the bodies of dead plants and animals down so that they rot away into the ground

digest   to break food up in the stomach

dissolve   to turn into liquid

energy   the power and goodness that living things need to keep their bodies working properly

fresh   fresh water is not salty

fungi   living things such as mushrooms, toadstools and moulds. Fungi are not animals or plants.

grasslands   huge, open spaces covered in grass and bushes

habitat   a particular place where plants and animals live

herbivore   an animal that only eats plants

hibernate   to go into a deep sleep-like state for winter

invertebrate   an animal that does not have a backbone or skeleton inside its body

krill   tiny, shrimp-like animals. They live in huge groups in the sea and are eaten by whales and other sea creatures.

larvae   the young of insects and some other animals

mammal   an animal such as an elephant, bat, horse and human

nitrate   a form of nitrogen found in the ground

nitrogen   a gas which living things need to grow

omnivore   an animal that eats both plants and animals

oxygen   a gas found in the air. Living things need to breathe oxygen to stay alive.

photosynthesis   the way green plants make their own food from sunlight, carbon dioxide and water

predator   an animal that hunts and kills other animals for food

prey   animals that are hunted and killed for food

primary consumer   an animal that feeds directly on plants. The word primary means first.

producers   green plants that produce or make their own food. They start off nearly every food chain.

pyramid of biomass a triangular shaped diagram which shows the total amount or weight of living things in a food chain

pyramid of numbers a triangular shaped diagram which shows the total number of each living thing in a food chain

rodent   an animal such as a rat, mouse and lemming

secondary consumer   an animal that feeds on animals that have eaten plants. The word secondary means second.

termite   a tiny insect that looks like an ant

Index